D1376359

# TOP STEM CAREERS IN TECHNOLOGY

LAURA LA BELLA

**ROSEN**
PUBLISHING®

New York

Published in 2015 by The Rosen Publishing Group, Inc.
29 East 21st Street, New York, NY 10010

First Edition

**Library of Congress Cataloging-in-Publication Data**

La Bella, Laura.
Top STEM careers in technology/Laura La Bella. — First edition.
    pages cm — (Cutting-edge STEM careers)
Audience: Grades 9-12.
Includes bibliographical references and index.
ISBN 978-1-4777-7668-1 (library bound) — ISBN 978-1-4777-7670-4 (pbk.) — ISBN 978-1-4777-7671-1 (6-pack)
1. Engineering—Vocational guidance—Juvenile literature. 2. Technology—Vocational guidance—Juvenile literature. I. Title.
TA157.L285 2015
602.3—dc23

                                        2013038825

*Manufactured in Malaysia*

# CONTENTS

In the near future, a tiny robot may have the ability to seek out and destroy cancer cells in the human body. These robots, called DNA nanorobots, are being development by biomedical engineers and technologists at Harvard University's Wyss Institute for Biologically Inspired Engineering. The nanorobots are microscopic in size and act as a delivery truck that can transport medication to specific cells in the human body. The goal is to enable these nanorobots to target malfunctioning cells and fix them when they break. It's an advancement in medicine that has the potential to change the way we treat cancer and other diseases. And it's the result of technology's impact on the field of science.

Careers in the STEM fields—science, technology, engineering, and mathematics—are driving the economy and redefining our way of life. STEM careers have influenced nearly every industry. Discoveries and innovations are changing how we treat environmental disasters, predict severe weather occurrences, develop medical devices, and collect and share data.

Students with an education in a STEM field can find amazing job opportunities. Currently there are more jobs available in the STEM field than there are candidates to fill them. These include positions that require only certification, vocational training, or an

Biomedical engineers have developed nanorobots that can be injected directly into the human body to seek out and deliver medication to specific cells.

associate's degree, as well as jobs that require a bachelor's or master's degree. There is a wide range of career options for students who have an interest in science, technology, engineering, and math.

STEM careers in technology span a wide range of interests. You can find a technology-related job in industries as diverse as animal care, chemistry, computing, engineering, health care, the environment, sustainability, and the sciences. No matter where your interests lie, if you like technology, you can find a career path to pursue.

# CHAPTER ONE

# Laying the Groundwork:
## Preparing for a STEM Career

Careers in the STEM disciplines—science, technology, engineering, and math—are projected to grow significantly over the next ten years. All around you, you'll find a connection to STEM. From science (the sun, moon, and stars; our oceans, weather, and natural disasters; animals, plant life, and food; fuel and wind power) and technology (the latest smartphones, flat screen TVs, and imaging systems) to engineering (roller coasters, roads, and appliances) to mathematics (banking, tax forms, and investments), STEM is everywhere you look.

Careers in the technology field are diverse. They span a wide rage of disciplines, including computing and software development, engineering technology, medicine, environmental health and sustainability, semiconductors, and science. It's an exciting field with a wide range of career paths and options for students who have an interest in technology and innovation.

Using dial tones, a physics class analyzes sound waves. Hands-on experiments illustrate for students the ways in which technology is used in the real world to solve problems.

## STEM Education: Keys to the Future

There is a push to recruit more students into STEM careers because the future outlook for STEM occupations

is staggeringly optimistic and promising. The U.S. Bureau of Labor Statistics projects that jobs in STEM fields are expected to grow by 17 percent by 2018. That's nearly double the rate of growth for non-STEM occupations. The U.S. Commerce Department also reports that those employed in the STEM fields now earn 26 percent higher wages than people employed in non-STEM professions. More significantly, STEM careers drive innovation, a key element of a successful economy and educated society.

Right now, there are thousands of STEM jobs that are unfilled. Why? Because high schools and colleges are not producing enough students with high skill levels in the competencies needed for success in these jobs. Education in the STEM disciplines is important for our nation's continued growth, prosperity, and global leadership.

STEM education is the preparation of students in competencies and skills in science, technology, engineering, and math. An effective, successful STEM education provides students with a wide range of course work in these disciplines. It also provides real-world situations in which students can learn to apply the knowledge they've acquired in the classroom. A solid STEM education not only instructs students in mathematics and science concepts, but also enables them to become critical thinkers and to see the potential in using science, technology, and engineering in new, exciting ways. Students who excel in the STEM disciplines are innovators, and innovation leads to new products and processes that build and support the economy.

When it comes to math and science, fourteen countries outperform U.S. students. Many of these nations are key leaders in technology and innovation. A recent ACT College and Career Readiness report found that only 29 percent of high school graduates are college-ready in science and 43 percent are college-ready in math. This educational gap has become a national problem. President Barack Obama has stated that the nation needs to require higher achievement in STEM education if it is to remain a leader in the future. During a speech at the National Academy of Sciences, President Obama said, "Reaffirming and strengthening America's role as the world's engine of scientific discovery and technological innovation is essential to meeting the challenges of this century."

As a result of the push toward creating stronger academic programs in the STEM disciplines, numerous programs have emerged to help schools and teachers better educate students in these areas. For example, Educate to Innovate is a ten-year campaign designed to increase science and math achievement. The campaign involves a partnership among major companies, universities, foundations, nonprofit organizations, and government agencies in an effort to improve education and create a pipeline of students who can excel in college-level programs that lead to STEM careers.

# Begin Your Technology Career in High School

For many students, serious focus on a career path begins in high school. Luckily, for those interested in the STEM fields, there is a wide range of regular class offerings and extracurricular clubs and activities that can get them started on developing their passion for technology.

High school students interested in the STEM fields should focus on completing regular high school–level courses in mathematics (algebra, precalculus, calculus, trigonometry, and geometry) and science (biology, chemistry, physics, and earth science). Participating in clubs—such as those that focus on the environment, mathematics, science, and technology—can help students gain an appreciation for how work in these fields affects our daily lives. They can also boost students' interest in pursuing career options within one of these fields.

Some schools offer engineering or technology-based courses through programs such as Project Lead the Way or Gateway to Technology. These kinds of programs help to develop students' innovative, collaborative, critical-thinking, and problem-solving skills through course work that provides an introduction to engineering and technology. Sample courses include: Introduction to Engineering, Principles of Engineering,

Engineering Design and Development, Automation and Robotics, Flight and Space, Science of Technology, and Green Architecture, to name a few.

In addition, there are multiple technology and engineering competitions that help students apply the concepts they are learning in the classroom to real-world problem solving. Some of the most well known are:

- **FIRST Robotics Competition:** For Inspiration and Recognition in Science and Technology (FIRST) is an international program for elementary through high school students. Using Legos, elementary participants solve real-world problems, while middle school students design and build robots to complete a specific task. High school students build fully functioning robots and compete in local, state, and national competitions. The program is designed to encourage students to use

Students participating in the 2006 FIRST Robotics Competition put the finishing touches on their team's robot in the pit area.

technology, engineering, math, and science to solve problems and accomplish tasks.

- **BEST Robotics:** Similar to FIRST Robotics, BEST (short for Boosting Engineering, Science, and Technology) competitions feature large, student-built robots designed to accomplish a specific task. Students work alongside professional engineers who serve as mentors and advisers.

- **National Science Bowl:** Hosted by the U.S. Department of Energy, the National Science Bowl is a nationwide academic competition that tests students' knowledge in all areas of science and technology. High school and middle school students are quizzed in a fast-paced question-and-answer format.

- **Invention Challenge:** The JPL (Jet Propulsion Laboratory) Annual Invention Challenge is a friendly competition designed to show students how fun math, science, technology, and engineering can be.

## Big Opportunities for Women and Minorities in STEM

Women and minorities are vastly underrepresented in the STEM fields. The National Science Foundation reports that while Caucasians represent 69 percent of working scientists and engineers, only 18 percent of STEM professionals are women, 18 percent are Asian, 5 percent are black, and 4 percent are Hispanic.

In general, women make up only 14 percent of the engineering, 23 percent of math and science, and 25 percent of professional information technology jobs. Minorities represent 28.5 percent of the U.S. population. They are the fastest growing segment of the

A girl test-drives a hovercraft built at a STEM summer camp in Belleville, Illinois. Camps such as these can help interest more women and minorities in STEM careers.

population. Yet they represent only 9.1 percent of college-educated Americans in the science and engineering workforce. Research, as well as discussions with middle and high school girls and minorities, has shown that more encouragement, relatable success stories, and hands-on activities can help inspire members of these underrepresented populations to seek a rewarding career path in one of the STEM fields.

Currently colleges and high schools are putting in more of an effort to encourage women and minorities

# ADVANCING WOMEN'S ROLES IN ENGINEERING

Many girls find that they are among a small handful of female students in their high school engineering, technology, or robotics classes. This can be discouraging for female students who have an interest in pursing engineering, technology, or other traditionally male-dominated career fields.

In order to counteract any shying away from these career fields, a number of organizations are reaching out to female middle and high school students, as well as female engineering majors enrolled in college programs, to encourage them to pursue a career path in the STEM disciplines. These organizations seek to inspire the next generation of female engineers through networking, outreach, and support.

## Society of Women Engineers

The Society of Women Engineers (SWE) is an organization that helps raise awareness of engineering careers for girls in middle and high school and helps to connect female college-aged engineering majors with professionals in the field.

For more than sixty years, SWE has given female engineers a voice within the male-dominated engineering and engineering technology fields. Most major universities with engineering and engineering technology programs host student chapters of SWE, where students connect with one another, network with professionals in the field, and assist in a growing number of outreach efforts aimed at engaging middle and high school girls in engineering and engineering technology. SWE also offers scholarship opportunities, continuing education opportunities such as conferences and seminars, and competitions and projects where students can show off their engineering skills.

## Nerd Girls

Nerd Girls is a growing global movement that celebrates the individuality and spirit of smart girls. The group encourages young women to embark on careers in the STEM disciplines while embracing their "girl power." The online community unites women, connects them with like-minded individuals, and offers mentoring and networking opportunities. Members of Nerd Girls also travel to college campuses and perform weekly outreach to middle and high school girls around the country.

## Women in Technology

Helping its members achieve their dreams is the purpose behind Women in Technology, a professional organization that understands the unique challenges facing women engineering and technology students. The group offers a wide range of programs, support, and resources to advance women in the technology fields. It offers programs addressing issues that professional women encounter on a daily basis, from balancing work and family and launching one's own business to taking charge of one's career and climbing the ladder to career success and professional and personal fulfillment.

to take science, technology, engineering, and math courses, as well as participate in STEM-related clubs and activities. Several national initiatives are also in place to help boost the interest of girls and minorities in these fields. They include:

- **Engineer Your Life:** This organization's website introduces high school girls to engineering careers. The site helps school counselors and teachers understand engineering and STEM-related fields and gives them resources and training in order to better advise female students who are considering careers in these fields.

- **National Society of Black Engineers' Summer Engineering Experience for Kids:** This free summer program invites three hundred African American students in the third through eighth grades to participate in camps held around the country. African American college students enrolled in STEM degree programs act as mentors and assist in hands-on projects and competitions using math, science, and problem-solving skills.

- **Nerd Girls Are Cool Too:** This is a growing movement by young women in the science and technology fields. According to its website, Nerd Girls wants to create a worldwide network that offers support and encouragement so that more girls will study STEM subjects in school and enter into what have historically been male-dominated professions.

In addition to summer camps and programs, several national organizations offer scholarships for women and minorities who enroll in college-level STEM programs. Among these are:

• Society of Hispanic Professional Engineers Foundation
• National Action Council for Minorities in Engineering
• National Association of Multicultural Engineering Program Advocates
• Organization of Black Aerospace Professionals
• Gates Millennium Scholars Program
• National Society of Black Physicists
• National Society of Black Engineers
• Society of Women Engineers
• The Center for Women in Technology
• Vanguard Women in Information Technology

## A Wide Range of Careers

When people think of STEM jobs, they typically think of engineers designing next-generation cars at one of the major automakers, a Web developer creating apps for smartphones, or a Silicon Valley entrepreneur raising capital for a new tech company. But those are only the high-profile careers.

According to the U.S. Bureau of Labor Statistics, nearly half of all high-tech positions are held by

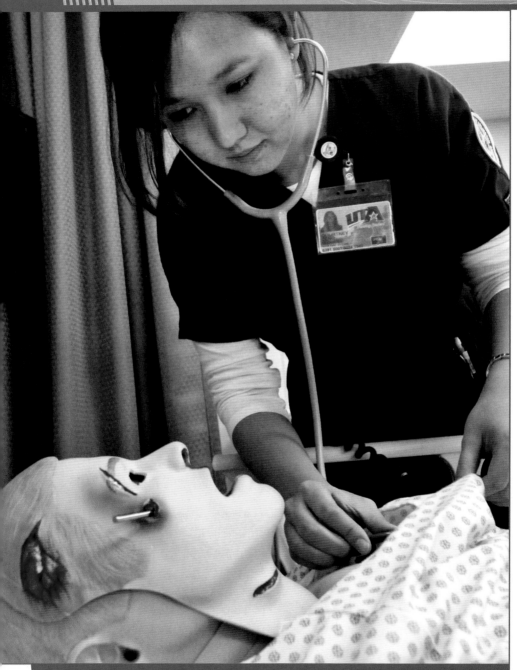

A Texas nursing student works with an interactive patient simulator. Nursing is among the most popular STEM careers that do not require a college degree.

employees who do not have a bachelor's degree. In fact, among the eight most popular STEM jobs that do not require a college degree, six pay more than the national annual average wage. Those jobs include registered nurses, automotive service technicians, carpenters, electricians, computer systems analysts, and machinists. While these jobs don't require a four-year college degree, they do have rigorous requirements. In addition, many have on-the-job training requirements or apprenticeships that take upward of five years to complete.

# CHAPTER TWO

# Building a Better Tomorrow:
## Engineering Technology

When Jordan Darling's Jet Ski experienced engine trouble on Lake Ontario last summer, he had to abandon ship. His personal watercraft sank in 8 feet (2.4 meters) of water, nearly 200 feet (61 m) from shore. It took Darling and his friends five days of searching to locate the vessel. The experience was an unlikely inspiration for Darling, who is a mechanical engineering technology major at Rochester Institute of Technology (RIT) in Rochester, New York. Darling used his skills in engineering and technology to create a prototype of a personal buoy that can be deployed to assist boaters in locating their sunken ships.

Darling's concept, called the Retriever, is a floatation pouch with a 50-foot (15-m) polypropylene rope coiled inside. The end of the rope is connected to the vehicle, and the pouch is secured with Velcro. Should a water-based vessel start to sink, the Retriever can be deployed. It leaves

Engineering technology is a field of study that focuses on practical instead of applied engineering skills.

the pouch floating on top of the water, making the locating and salvaging of the sunken vessel far easier.

## What Is Engineering Technology?

Engineering technology is a field of study that focuses on engineering skills that are more practical than applied in nature. The Accreditation Board for Engineering and Technology (ABET), which accredits undergraduate and graduate degree programs in engineering, technology, and computing, defines an engineering technology program as one that focuses on practical application and implementation. In comparison, most other engineering programs are focused more on theory and conceptual design.

There are two-year engineering technology programs available at community colleges and technical schools and four-year degree programs at colleges and universities. Graduates of four-year engineering technology programs earn a bachelor of science (B.S.) degree in a particular area of engineering technology. These professionals are called technologists. Graduates of two-year engineering technology programs earn an associate of applied science (A.A.S.) degree in a particular area of engineering technology and are referred to as technicians. In addition, some community colleges offer a two-year certificate program in engineering technology.

Professionals who earn a degree in engineering technology are most likely to enter careers in fields as diverse as construction, manufacturing, industrial or product design, product development, product testing, technical service and sales, and facilities management.

There is a wide range of disciplines within the engineering technology field. Types of engineering technology subfields include biomedical engineering technology, civil engineering technology, computer engineering technology, electrical engineering technology, electrical/mechanical engineering technology, industrial engineering technology, manufacturing engineering technology, and mechanical engineering technology.

# Engineering Technology Jobs

With so many areas of engineering technology to choose from, a wide range of jobs are available. Below is a sample of popular career paths one may pursue in the engineering technology field.

## Surveyors

*Job Description:* Surveyors establish land, airspace, and water boundaries by measuring the earth's surface to collect data, draw maps, and determine the shape and size of parcels of land. They also define airspace for airports and measure construction and mining sites.

*Duties and Responsibilities:* Surveyors measure distances, directions, and angles between points on, above, and below the earth's surface. They select known reference points to determine the exact location of a boundary of land or water. They research land records, identify previous boundaries to determine current boundaries, and travel to various locations to measure distances and directions between points. Surveyors record the results of their work and verify the accuracy of their data. They also prepare plots of land, draw maps, and issue reports.

*Work Environment:* The majority of surveyors work for architectural and engineering firms. They work in offices as well as in the field, where they conduct their assessments and take measurements. Surveyors usually work full time and most often work longer hours during the summer months when warmer weather allows for construction projects to take place.

*Educational Requirements:* Surveyors typically need a bachelor's degree in a field such as civil engineering technology, surveying technology, forestry, or a related program of study. These programs include course work in surveying, construction, computer-aided drafting, civil engineering graphics, field orientation and measurements, spatial analysis of natural resources, environmental modeling, and soils and hydrology.

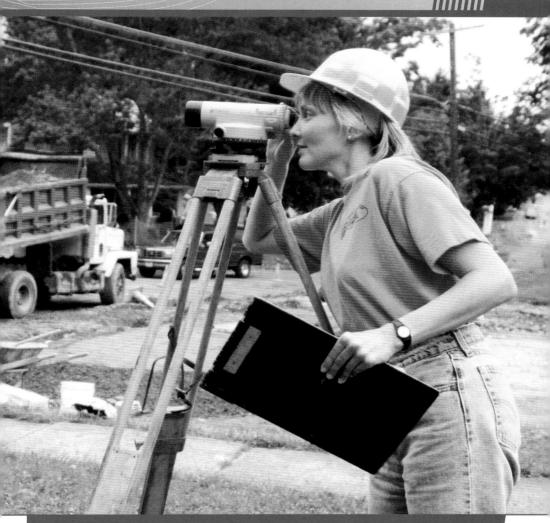

Surveyors work on construction sites to establish land, air, and water boundaries.

*Additional Skills:* Surveyors should be detail oriented, have strong mathematical skills, and be adept at problem solving. Visualization skills are very important, as surveyors must be able to envision objects, distances, and sizes.

*Certifications/Licensures:* All fifty states and the District of Columbia require surveyors to be licensed. Only licensed surveyors can determine proper markings on construction projects and sites or legally certify documents that show property lines. To become a licensed surveyor, you must complete the highest level of education required by your state, gain experience under a licensed surveyor, and pass two exams (the Fundamentals of Surveying Exam and the Principles and Practice of Surveying Exam).

*Internships Opportunities:* Surveyors.com is an industry website that features internship opportunities in a wide range of work settings, including architecture firms, engineering firms, government agencies, real estate, mining companies, and more. The work will vary depending on the company, but typically interns complete basic tasks and assist a licensed surveyor in the field.

# Biomedical Engineers

*Job Description:* A biomedical engineer analyzes and designs solutions to problems in biology and medicine, with the goal of improving the quality and effectiveness of patient care.

*Duties and Responsibilities:* Biomedical engineers design devices, such as artificial organs and joints, which can replace ailing body parts. They also design and develop machines for diagnosing medical problems, as well as install, maintain, or repair this equipment. Biomedical engineers evaluate biomedical equipment and test its effectiveness. They may also train technicians and other medical personnel on the proper use and handling of this equipment.

*Work Environment:* Depending on what they do, biomedical engineers can work in a wide variety of settings. Some are employed by hospitals where they oversee medical equipment. Others work in manufacturing settings where they develop medical equipment and biomedical devices. Many work in laboratories performing research and product development.

*Educational Requirements:* Biomedical engineers need a bachelor's degree in biomedical engineering technology or a related field. These programs combine courses in engineering and technology with those in the biological sciences. Typical courses in these programs may include analytical chemistry, physics, anatomy and physiology, cellular and molecular biology, musculoskeletal biomechanics, biomedical device engineering, biomaterials, and biomedical signal processing.

*Additional Skills:* Biomedical engineers need to have good analytical skills as they determine the needs of both patients and medical professionals. They must be good listeners, have exceptional mathematical skills, and be able to solve complex problems involving the human body and its systems.

*Internships/Co-op Opportunities:* Internships and co-ops are available to college-level students who are completing degree programs in biomedical engineering technology and biomedical technology. These opportunities are available at manufacturing and pharmaceutical companies where devices or medical equipment

A biomedical software engineer reviews a three-dimensional brain scan used by surgeons with a patient and his parents. Biomedical engineers are the minds behind several innovative medical advancements.

are being developed and in hospitals where equipment is used, installed, or in need of maintenance.

*Career Advancement:* Biomedical engineers who have worked in the field for several years and have

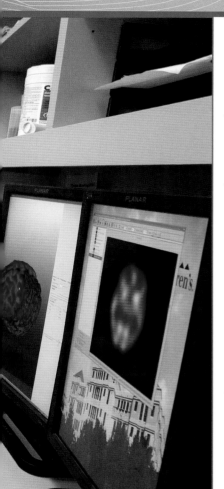

gained significant professional experience may become leaders of research teams. For these jobs, advanced degrees are required. A master's degree in a related biomedical field or in business administration can provide the necessary skills in personnel, management, and project leadership. Some biomedical engineers attend dental or medical school in order to specialize in developing devices for dental or surgical applications. Some pursue a law degree and work in patent law, which is helpful for those professionals who develop new and emerging biomedical technologies.

## Industrial Production Managers

*Job Description:* Industrial production managers oversee the daily operations of manufacturing plants. They coordinate, plan, and direct the activities used to create a wide range of consumer products, including cars, electronic equipment, computer equipment, and paper products.

*Duties and Responsibilities:* Depending on the size of the plant, industrial production managers might oversee the entire plant or just one section of it. Their daily duties include deciding how best to use a plant's workers and equipment to meet production goals. They monitor production to remain on schedule and on budget. They hire, train, and evaluate the performance of production workers. Industrial production managers also analyze production data and information, oversee plant safety requirements, monitor equipment, decide when upgrades or newer machinery is needed, and troubleshoot and solve problems.

*Work Environment:* Most industrial production managers split their time between the production floor and their office. While working near or on machinery, industrial production managers are required to wear protective clothing such as hard hats, gloves, and goggles. Industrial production managers work full time and can work a variety of hours, including nights and weekends, to accommodate production deadlines or to meet supply and demand.

*Educational Requirements:* To work as an industrial production manager, you will need a bachelor's degree in industrial engineering technology, manufacturing engineering technology, or a related field. These programs cover topics such as manufacturing processes, mechanical design and fabrication, materials in engineering, automation control systems, electronics manufacturing, robotics and automation, lean production, supply chain operations, and integrated design for manufacturing and assembly. Because this position includes management responsibilities, additional courses in business, managerial skills, human resources, or leadership can prove valuable.

## THE TEN TOP-RANKED UNIVERSITIES THAT GRANT THE MOST STEM DEGREES

*(source: U.S. News & World Report)*

| School | Percentage of bachelor's degrees granted in STEM disciplines (2012) | National rank |
|---|---|---|
| California Institute of Technology | 98% | 10 |
| Colorado School of Mines | 98% | 77 |
| Missouri University of Science and Technology | 91% | 125 |
| Worcester Polytechnic Institute | 88% | 65 |
| Massachusetts Institute of Technology | 86% | 65 |
| Rensselaer Polytechnic Institute | 84% | 41 |
| Stevens Institute of Technology | 82% | 75 |
| Michigan Technological University | 77% | 120 |
| Clarkson University | 76% | 115 |
| Georgia Institute of Technology | 76% | 39 |

Training: Many industrial production managers spend the first few months of their employment in training programs at their companies. These programs allow trainees to become familiar with the production process, company policies, and safety regulations. Once oriented to the company and its work, industrial production managers begin working on a production line to gain experience through hands-on work.

Gay Terry is the first female industrial plant manager for Delphi Energy and Chassis Systems in Saginaw, Michigan. She oversees the manufacture of more than sixty-five thousand car brakes a day.

*Certifications:* Certification for industrial production managers is optional and not a requirement for employment. However, the Association for Operations Management offers a certification in Production and Inventory Management (CPIM) credential, while the American Society for Quality offers credentials in quality control.

*Career Advancement:* Larger production plants with managers who have significant oversight and responsibilities may seek out candidates who have earned a master of business administration (MBA) or a graduate degree in industrial management. These programs provide focused curriculum in management, production systems, production technology, innovation, and leadership.

## Automotive Service Technician

*Job Description:* Automotive service technicians inspect, maintain, and repair cars and trucks. As the automobile industry continues to integrate computing technology and advanced electrical systems into vehicles, automotive service technicians now need to be familiar with those electronic systems and computing components that control a vehicle's ability to brake and steer.

*Duties and Responsibilities:* Automotive service technicians use computerized diagnostic equipment to identify mechanical problems. They test parts and systems to ensure that they are working correctly. They maintain a vehicle's engine and perform care and maintenance on a vehicle's other components. They may replace brake pads, perform tune-ups, rotate tires, disassemble and reassemble parts, and use testing equipment to ensure repairs are made accurately.

*Work Environment:* The vast majority of automotive service technicians work in repair shops or in the service department of dealerships. These are often well-lit, well-ventilated spaces specifically designed for automotive care and service. Technicians work weekends and evenings. Overtime is common.

An automotive technician uses a hand held computer to diagnose a car he is servicing. Technicians use advanced techological tools to work on computerized automotive systems.

*Educational Requirements:* Completing a vocational or training program in automotive service technology is the best preparation for entry-level positions. These programs typically provide six to twelve months of intensive classroom instruction and hands-on practice. Some service technicians earn a two-year associate's degree in automotive technology or mechanical technology. These programs include hands-on work in automotive repairs and maintenance along with coursework in basic mathematics, computers, and electronics.

*Required Training:* Most automotive service technicians complete on-the-job training where they learn the specific care and service requirements for different models of cars and trucks. It takes two to five years of experience before you can become a fully qualified service technician.

*Certification:* A certification in one of eight areas (automatic transmission/transaxle, brakes, electrical/electronic systems, engine performance, engine repair, heating and air-conditioning, manual drive train and axles, and suspension and steering) is the standard for employment in the field. Certifications can be obtained through the National Institute for Automotive Service Excellence (ASE).

# CHAPTER THREE

# Wrap It Up!
## Packaging Science

The Otterbox is among the best-selling smartphone cases on the market. It encloses smartphones in a hard polycarbonate inner layer that is itself encased in a soft silicon outer layer. According to its website, the Otterbox will protect smartphones against a 10-foot (3-m) drop onto concrete, two tons of crushing force, and underwater submersion in 6 feet (1.8 m) of water for up to thirty minutes. Whereas it can cost several hundred dollars to replace a broken smartphone, a case that prevents damage to either the phone or its data is well worth the far smaller price of investment.

The Otterbox is more than just a protective cover for smartphones, however. It's also an example of effective packaging design. Packaging can do everything from keeping electronics safe and food fresh to communicating product warnings and usage instructions. Packaging science

Packaging scientists were behind the invention of the hot-selling Otterbox, made by one of the nation's largest manufacturers of protective cases for mobile devices.

is an exciting career path that allows you to design and develop packaging solutions for a wide range of manufacturing and consumer needs and concerns.

## What Is Packaging Science?

Packaging is everywhere. Just search the aisles of the local supermarket to get an idea of how extensive

A milk jug looks simple. Yet packaging scientists have designed and tested ways to use the best materials to ensure that milk maintains its freshness and quality during shipping and use.

the field of packaging is. The plastic wrapping around frozen pizza eliminates moisture and helps it stay fresh longer. Milk retains its nutritional value thanks to its white plastic bottle, which prevents exposure to light and the resulting nutrient depletion.

Packaging is a combination of the science, art, engineering, and technology of encasing or protecting products for distribution, shipping, storage, and sale. Every single retail item is packaged in some way— from lipstick and juice boxes to flat screen TVs and contact lens. The people behind the design of these containers are packaging scientists.

Packaging is more than the box or carton a product comes in. It also includes bottles, cans, wrappers, cartons, shrink and bubble wrap, packing "peanuts," and envelopes. Packaging scientists use a wide variety of materials to tackle the issues and challenges associated with packaging, shipping, and displaying products. They look for ways to safely store and package products, to ship items in ways that eliminate damage, and to develop packaging materials that won't harm the environment. In addition to focusing upon the functionality of packaging, these professionals also create packaging designs that entice the consumer, help advertise and sell products, and provide important consumer information.

# Packaging Is Important

The main purpose of packaging is to protect the products contained inside, but packaging accomplishes much more than that. There are so many ways in which packaging is used to provide benefits to the consumer:

- **Physical protection:** The objects enclosed in a package may need protection from shock, vibration, dust, water, oxygen, moisture, air, or other damaging elements.

- **Containment:** Small objects are typically grouped together in one package to make shipping and selling more convenient. A package of ten pens requires less materials and handling and is easier to display in a store than are ten individual pens.

- **Information and communication:** Packaging often informs consumers about how to use a product, what it does, or what it is made of. Food packaging includes cooking instructions. Product packaging communicates the value, uses, or benefits of a product. Medical packaging tells us how often and in what dosage we should consume medicine.

- **Marketing:** Packaging is an opportunity to set products apart from one another on store shelves. Two coffeemakers may look the same, but effective packaging and marketing can illustrate the benefits of one product over another.

- **Safety and security:** Tamper-resistant caps on medicine are one example of how packaging increases the safety of a product. Antitheft devices within packaging can deter theft and shoplifting of expensive items

- **Convenience:** Single-use food items, individual-serving frozen meals, and resealable bags are all examples of packaging that increases the convenience of use for consumers.

- **Portion control:** A single-serve package of cookies or a single-dose capsule of medicine can help consumers gauge portion control or assist them in measuring the correct, safe, or recommended amount of a product.

# An Education in Packaging

Careers in packaging science begin with a foundation of course work in science and mathematics. These courses can be completed in high school and can include classes in physics, chemistry, and mathematics (algebra, precalculus, and calculus). Some high schools offer courses in engineering design, graphic design, illustration, and drawing. Any additional courses in these subject areas will further prepare you for advanced study in packaging programs at technical and vocational schools, two-year associate degree programs at community colleges, or four-year bachelor's degree programs at colleges and universities.

For students who attend technical, trade, or vocational schools, programs in manufacturing automation, motion control, or fluid power technology can help prepare you for packaging jobs that do not require a college degree. These programs focus on topics such as hydraulics, pneumatics, electricity, electronics, robotics, and automation. Students learn functional knowledge that is useful for basic jobs in manufacturing or on an assembly line where packaging materials are produced.

Two-year associate's degrees in packaging science, engineering science, commercial art, or graphic design can provide a foundation of skills for those who wish to enter the workforce after two years of college-level course work. Packaging science and engineering science programs will provide students

Laura Knoll (*center*), a packaging science major at the University of Florida's Institute of Food and Agricultural Sciences, uses a computer-aided design table to assemble a point-of-purchase display she designed.

with a background in the fundamentals of engineering, packaging and engineering materials, and manufacturing and assembly line production. Programs in commercial art or graphic design will introduce students to foundational art and drawing, design techniques, color and color theory, two-dimensional design, computer graphics, and photography.

Most packaging jobs require a bachelor's degree in packaging science, packaging engineering, or packaging design. These programs identify the strategic issues involved in creating the packaging for a company or brand. They incorporate technological innovations and focus on engineering principles for manufacturing, materials, and production. Course work covers topics such as materials, food and health packaging, packaging design and graphics, chemical processes and applications, packaging metals and plastics, packaging paper and glass, packaging for distribution and shipping, packaging regulations, and protective packaging.

## A Career in Packaging

Packaging is a $100 billion a year industry. It's the third largest industry in the United States and is expected to grow rapidly as more and more companies focus their

UPS packaging engineer Preeti Agrawal tests the integrity of a shipping box at the company's testing lab in Addison, Illinois. Overseeing testing procedures is part of a packaging engineer's job.

efforts on creating sustainable or environmentally friendly packaging solutions. It's also a large career field that spans engineering, design, marketing, production, research, and development.

With such diversity in job opportunities and career paths, a career in packaging is ever-changing and evolving. Both consumer companies and production and manufacturing facilities employ packaging scientists and packaging designers. You can work for a company that specializes in manufacturing of packages for other companies, or you may work for a consumer product company and work on specific kinds of packaging. Each area needs individuals who are professionally trained in the wide-ranging aspects of the packaging industry.

## Packaging Engineers

*Job Description:* Packaging engineers are responsible for developing packaging for a company's products. They also choose the packaging materials, develop new materials, and design and develop the machinery that produces packaging supplies.

*Duties and Responsibilities:* Packaging engineers collect and analyze data from suppliers and consumers, design and execute experiments to test new packaging ideas, implement improvements or corrections to packaging, manage changes to testing procedures, assist in selecting suppliers for packaging materials, and negotiate supplier costs.

*Work Environment:* Many packaging engineers work in manufacturing settings and solve packaging

## PACKAGING DESIGN AT WORK: HEINZ REDESIGNS THE KETCHUP PACKET

The ketchup packet was created in 1968 and hadn't undergone any major design changes in the years since. The packet made using ketchup on the go far easier, neater, and more convenient. Yet it still wasn't very easy to tear open and didn't account for eating in the car or dunking French fries. Product designers at Heinz found that while the ketchup packet worked well at the table, it didn't work well anywhere else.

In response to consumer complaints, Heinz gathered a team of packaging designers. The company also surveyed consumers to get their thoughts on how they wanted to see the packaging improved. Drivers wanted something that could sit on the armrest or in the cup holder. Passengers wanted the choice of either squeezing or dunking. Moms wanted a packet that held enough ketchup for the meal but didn't squirt so easily onto clothes.

Heinz bought a used minivan, and the design team went to work testing out new designs and experimenting with them to test the effectiveness in a real-world setting. The result was the idea for the dip and squeeze packet. Consumers can now tear off a cap to squeeze their ketchup onto food or they can peel off the seal to dunk their food into the ketchup.

problems on the assembly line. They work with engineers, manufacturing and production experts, and project managers as they determine the best ways to package a product.

*Educational Requirements:* Packaging engineers typically hold a bachelor's degree in packaging engineering, manufacturing engineering, systems engineering, or a related subject. Academic programs in these areas include course work in topics such as chemistry, materials processing, production and supply chain operations, manufacturing and assembly design, engineering management, facilities planning, and manufacturing.

# Packaging Designers

*Job Description:* A packaging designer works with clients and creative teams to develop attractive, efficient, and cost-effective packaging for products. They usually brainstorm, sketch, and create design concepts based on the sales and marketing goals of their client and the packaging needs of the product.

*Duties and Responsibilities:* Packaging designers are often part of a marketing team, which is responsible for raising awareness of a product and communicating its value to the consumer. Packaging designers meet with clients to develop an understanding of the product, its benefits, and how it is different than similar products on the market. They take this information and begin to conceptualize and design ideas for the product's packaging. They share these ideas with the client and work to adjust the design based on the client's feedback. Packaging designers may also meet with engineers to ensure their packaging successfully encloses the product, with accounting professionals to make sure their design is cost effective, and with sustainability or environmental safety groups to ensure the packaging does not harm the environment and meets recycling standards.

*Work Environment:* Packaging designers can work for a consumer product company or for a design or advertising firm. They work in offices and spend much of their day designing on a computer using graphic design software. They work with a wide variety of people, from other designers and packaging engineers to copywriters and clients, as they develop effective packaging designs.

*Educational Requirements:* Most entry-level positions require a bachelor's degree in industrial design, packaging science, graphic design, or a related field. These programs include course work in areas such as art, graphic design, typography, color theory, design imagery, design production, information design, product design theory, and product design creation. Additional course work is focused on marketing principles, buyer behavior, sustainability, and commerce.

# Packaging Internships and Co-ops

To make yourself marketable, an internship or co-op in packaging gives you the hands-on experience you'll need to set yourself apart from the crowd of other applicants. Internships and co-ops allow you to gain experience working on real-world packaging projects where you can solve an issue for a company and be a part of a team of professionals working on the latest packaging innovations. As an intern or co-op participant, you'll be assigned activities where you may develop pallets, create displays for large brands, or research and troubleshoot problems. You'll also get an inside look at how companies develop and implement cost-saving or environmentally friendly packaging solutions.

Packaging internships or co-ops can be obtained by going directly to the websites of product companies or by going to industry-wide employment sites, such as PackagingCareers.com. This site lists open positions for internships, co-ops, and full-time employment for those with a background in packaging science, packaging design, or other areas of the packaging field.

# CHAPTER FOUR

# Go Green!
## Technology and the Environment

Technology has had a powerful impact upon our environment, both positively and negatively. Fossil fuels and nonrenewable energy sources, construction, land use, pollution, and more all impact the quality of our water and air, deplete our natural resources, and contribute to global warming. While we need technology to construct buildings, engineer roadways, facilitate and expedite transportation, and deliver goods and services, we also need to find ways to lessen the impact of these activities on the environment.

Careers in environmental health, sustainability, and pollution prevention are growing in both need and popularity and are rooted in the STEM disciplines. Environmental management is all about monitoring the use of natural resources, examining the short- and long-term impact of human activity associated with particular projects, and identifying solutions and strategies to lessen or eliminate any damage or harm to the environment incurred by this activity.

# Environmental Technology Careers

Cleaning up the environment, creating ways to reduce waste, and establishing safe and environmentally friendly workplaces is a priority. In the past, before environmental regulations were established, many companies would dump chemicals and other pollutants into waterways and landfills. Environmental disasters have damaged our natural resources and decimated many plant and animal populations. Natural disasters like hurricanes and earthquakes have created numerous crisis situations in which salvage and rebuilding efforts must be undertaken in order to return communities to their original state.

Environmental remediation is the removal of pollutants, chemicals, and other toxic contaminants from water, air, and the soil. These waste products need to be removed for the protection of human, animal, and plant life and to reduce damage to the environment or restore it to health. Environmental remediation projects can range from large, expensive projects—such as the containment and collection of oil spills in a large body of water or revitalizing soil after an underground chemical leak—to the cleaning up of chemical spills on a highway following trucking accidents. It can also mean removing debris from structures damaged during natural disasters such as earthquakes and hurricanes.

A geologic engineer inspects a barrier installed at the Concord Naval Weapons Station. The barrier is intended to keep contamination from flowing off the base into surrounding wetlands.

A relatively new career path in environmental technology is sustainability. According to the Environmental Protection Agency (EPA), sustainability "creates and maintains the conditions under which humans and nature can exist in productive harmony." It ensures that, as we consume and use our natural resources, we do so in a responsible manner. For example, as trees are cut down to manufacture paper, additional trees are planted immediately to replace them. New construction makes use of solar energy panels to power the structure, and sustainable or "green" products, such as Sheetrock and paint, are used to lessen the new building's carbon footprint.

# Environmental Engineering Technicians

*Job Description:* Environmental engineering technicians carry out cleanup plans created by environmental engineers. They test and operate equipment during the cleanup, collect and test water and soil, and work to eliminate sources of pollution.

*Duties and Responsibilities:* Environmental engineering technicians set up and operate equipment used for cleaning up environmental disasters. They collect and test water, air, and soil samples before, during, and after cleanup and maintain records of test results. They identify the source of the pollution and work to eliminate further contamination. Environmental engineering technicians also schedule cleanup activities, ensure that cleanup procedures meet safety requirements, and arrange for the removal of hazardous materials.

*Work Environment:* The majority of environmental engineering technicians work for management, technical, or consulting firms that specialize in environmental remediation and cleanup. They work both at the site of a cleanup and in labs where they conduct testing on samples collected at the polluted site. These technicians can work with dangerous materials and must follow safety regulations. These can include wearing protective gear (helmets, hazmat suits, goggles, masks).

*Educational Requirements:* While environmental engineering technicians do not need an associate's degree, many employers prefer candidates who have earned one or have completed college-level courses in the field. Students should focus on taking as many math and science courses as possible in high school. Courses in earth science are especially helpful. For those interested in attending college or taking college-level classes, course work in engineering technology, environmental safety, hazardous materials, and environmental biology are especially useful.

An EPA worker retrieves samples for water testing. Environmental technologists determine the extent of environmental damage and how best to proceed with remediation efforts.

*Additional Skills:* Environmental engineering technicians should be detail-oriented and have exceptional monitoring skills. They must properly evaluate a site and recognize problems quickly, as environmental pollutants can spread at rapid rates. They must also be able to read and comprehend legal and technical documents related to local, state, and federal regulations. Technicians must also be able to work both independently and on teams.

*Career Advancement:* Environmental engineering technicians usually begin as entry-level trainees who are supervised by an environmental engineer or a more experienced technician. As they gain experience both on-site and in labs, technicians will be assigned more responsibility and will be asked to carry out increasingly complicated assignments. After gaining sufficient experience, technicians can be promoted to supervisory positions. For those with a bachelor's degree, career advancement can include engineering and management positions.

# Environmental Scientists and Specialists

*Job Description:* Environmental scientists and specialists have extensive knowledge of the environmental and natural sciences. They use this knowledge to protect the environment by identifying problems and finding solutions that ensure the health of the environment.

*Duties and Responsibilities:* Environmental scientists and specialists analyze environmental problems and develop solutions by collecting data, conducting

# GREEN SMART HOMES

Green building—the design and construction of homes and commercial businesses using environmentally friendly methods, systems, and materials—is among the biggest trends in construction. With energy prices expected to continue to rise, people are looking for ways to build homes that take advantage of energy conservation techniques.

Many common building materials either contain substances harmful to our health or they release toxic and carcinogenic substances when they are manufactured. A large part of green building focuses on identifying and using natural resources (such as wind, sun, and rainwater) or using less harmful alternatives to products that contain harmful substances. For example, there is now plywood made without formaldehyde-based glues, natural fiber-based insulation instead of fiberglass, and bamboo-based products in place of tropical hardwoods. By using these alternative materials, we can reduce our carbon footprint as well as save natural resources, such as wood and lumber.

A second significant aspect of green building is the promotion of greater energy efficiency. Using insulation to prevent drafts and promote cooling in summer and heating in winter lessens the use of air conditioners and heating systems, and therefore the energy and natural resources required to power them. Green buildings also use the sun and wind as renewable alternative energy sources. They feature more efficient roofing and energy systems that use the sun and wind to generate heat and power in place of using electricity, gas, or oil.

Homes built using green practices can be certified as "LEED for Homes," the industry gold standard for sustainable construction. LEED certification (short for Leadership in Energy and Environmental Design) was once limited to only commercial construction projects. But LEED has now added homes to its rating system, which verifies for homeowners that their houses meet certain environmentally friendly building and material regulations.

In addition to green construction, many homes are now using smart technology (also called home automation) to operate their living spaces. Smart homes connect devices such as lights, thermostats, televisions, appliances, security systems, and more to remote controls, smartphones, tablets, or computers, allowing the home owner to control his or her living space from anywhere. Smart homes allow you to lower the temperature of your home to conserve energy on a warm day, turn off lights when no one is home, and control your home security system while you're on the go.

If you are miles away from home, and the sun suddenly comes out or the air temperature rises, you can use a digital device to lower your home's thermostat. Or, if you are on your way home, after being out all day, you can use your smartphone or tablet to preheat the oven, turn on the outdoor lights, and turn on the air-conditioning, so everything will be ready and comfortable upon your return. This is an exciting and effective new way to help control the energy efficiency of your home when you are not actively using your living space.

research, and performing investigations. They collect samples of water, air, soil, and other materials for analysis and testing. They analyze these samples to identify damage or threats of damage to the environment. They create plans to prevent, control, or fix and remediate environmental problems. They also record information and present their findings to officials at local, state, and federal environmental agencies.

*Work Environment:* The majority of environmental scientists work for local, state, or federal government agencies or environmental consulting firms. They spend time in the field monitoring environmental conditions and gathering data and work in offices and labs where they analyze the data and write reports.

*Educational Requirements:* For most jobs in this field, a bachelor's degree in environmental science, natural science, biology, or a related field is required. These programs provide a comprehensive understanding of the environment and its ecosystems. Course work includes topics such as ecology and field biology, environmental health, biological systems, environmental health and risk assessment, environmental chemistry, biodiversity, environmental disasters, environmental field skills, environmentalism, and conservation.

*Additional Skills:* Because environmental scientists base their conclusions on the analysis of data, strong analytical and decision-making skills are necessary for success in this field. Problem-solving and communication skills are also essential, as information must be shared with internal and external groups.

*Career Advancement:* Environmental scientists and specialists often begin their careers as field analysts, research assistants, or technicians. As they gain experience in the field, supervisors will assign them more responsibility. Environmental scientists and specialists can grow in their careers to become project leaders or managers or move into research positions.

# Health and Safety Engineers

*Job Description:* Health and safety engineers investigate accidents, injuries, or occupational diseases that occur at a work site. They work to determine the causes of the injury or illness and try to identify if it could have been prevented. This field, called environmental health and safety, encompasses both people and facilities.

*Duties and Responsibilities:* Health and safety engineers are responsible for creating procedures and developing systems to keep people from getting sick or injured on a job site and to keep property and machinery from being damaged. They review the specifications for new machinery or equipment to make sure it meets or exceeds safety regulations. They inspect work sites to identify potential hazards and ensure that buildings and equipment comply with state and federal health and safety regulations. They also establish or review employee safety programs and make recommendations on ways to improve safety at a work site.

*Work Environment:* Typically, health and safety engineers work in offices but spend some of their time at work sites observing employee behavior, equipment use, and how well safety regulations are being observed. Most health and safety engineers work in

OSHA officials inspect the site of a collapsed casino in Cincinnati, Ohio, in 2012. Health and safety engineers determine how such events happened and if they could have been prevented.

manufacturing and production facilities where large equipment is used.

*Educational Requirements:* Health and safety engineers must have a bachelor's degree in an engineering or engineering technology field, such as electrical, chemical, mechanical, or industrial engineering. These four-year programs provide an understanding of the manufacturing and production processes used in plants that create or produce products. Course work is heavily centered on math, engineering, and technology. Classes cover subjects such as environmental health, hazardous materials, occupational safety, industrial waste management, accident causation and prevention, organizational behavior, environmental health and safety law, and worker safety.

*Required Skills and Training:* Students interested in becoming health and safety engineers should seek out additional course work in occupational safety and health, industrial hygiene, or ergonomics. Computer skills are also used widely in this field.

*Certifications/Licensures:* While there are no certifications or licensure required in this field, students should seek our degree programs accredited by the Accreditation Board for Engineering and Technology (ABET).

*Internships/Co-op Opportunities:* Employers value practical experience, so students should seek out internship or co-op opportunities where they can gain hands-on experience. Co-op and internship opportunities are widely available at companies that manufacture or produce consumer or business products.

# Hydrologists

*Job Description:* Hydrologists study water and the water cycle. They monitor the movement, distribution, and other properties of water, and they analyze how water influences the surrounding environment.

*Duties and Responsibilities:* Hydrologists measure water properties, collect water and soil samples to test for pollutants, and analyze their findings. They research and develop methods for water conservation and pollution prevention and use computer models to

Hydrologists conduct tests and analyze how water affects the surrounding environment. They are key to developing pollution prevention programs.

forecast water supply and the spread of pollution and other potentially hazardous environmental damage.

*Work Environment:* The federal government and engineering firms employ the greatest number of hydrologists. Like other occupations in the environmental health field, hydrologists work both on-site collecting data and in offices analyzing information and drafting reports.

*Educational Requirements:* For most jobs, hydrologists need a master's degree in environmental science, engineering technology, environmental health, or a related field. There are very few degree programs in hydrology; however, many related programs have concentrations or minors in water resources or wastewater management.

*Certifications/Licensures:* In some states, hydrologists need a license to practice. Requirements vary by state, but typically they include a minimum level of education, a certain amount of on-the-job experience, and the successful passing of an exam.

# Entering the Digital Realm:
## Computers, Software, and Information Technology

A career in computer science opens the door to a multitude of opportunities. All businesses and industries need people who have a background in computer science, information technology, or software development. Businesses need websites, digital infrastructure, and connectivity. An education in computing provides students with the problem-solving and reasoning skills that they need to create innovative software, devise interactive games, build massive databases, or design and program the computers that are now used in nearly all types of products, from coffeemakers to cars.

## Computing Careers

Computing technology is everywhere you look. And careers in computing span all industries. No matter where your interests lie—education, gaming, health care, engineering communication and media, law, or economics—there are computing jobs available. Computing makes things happen. Computer programming provides the instructions that make it possible for machinery to accomplish desired tasks.

## Medical Records and Health Information Technicians

*Job Description:* Medical records and health information technicians organize and manage health information

Computers have changed the way medical information is collected, stored, studied, and used. Health information organization and management is vital to ensuring accuracy and comprehensive patient care.

by ensuring its accuracy, accessibility, and security. Instead of providing patient care, these technicians take care of your medical records to make sure your medical history, symptoms, test results, and treatments are documented correctly and available for review by doctors in your health system.

*Duties and Responsibilities:* Medical records and health information technicians review patient records and organize the data for easy accessibility. They develop and implement an organizational system so that data can be analyzed and reported. Using computer programming codes, they enable data to be retrieved and stored. They also create security protocols to ensure your medical information remains confidential.

*Work Environment:* Most medical records and health information technicians work in hospitals or in physician offices where patient information—such as tests, treatments, and test results—is used most actively. These professionals work full time and may work evenings or weekends.

*Educational Requirements:* Medical records and health information technicians typically need a post-secondary certificate. Some may have an associate's degree. Typically, students obtain a certificate or associate's degree in health information technology. This program usually covers courses in medical terminology, anatomy and physiology, health data requirements, classification and coding systems, health care reimbursement methods, health care statistics, computer programming, and computer systems.

*Required Skills and Training:* Strong familiarity with medical terminology and basic medical procedures is helpful to understand the data being compiled and produced by health care databases. Medical records and health information technicians must also be detailed oriented to ensure medical information is accurate. Misinformation can result in poor analysis results, inappropriate treatments, and potential harm to the patient.

*Certifications/Licensures:* Many employers require professional certification as a registered health information technician (RHIT) or certified tumor registrar (CTR). Requirements for these certifications vary by state.

# Computer Systems Analysts

*Job Description:* Computer systems analysts study a company's computer systems and procedures. They make recommendations on how an organization can operate more efficiently and effectively. This field is a combination of business and information technology.

*Duties and Responsibilities:* Computer systems analysts work with a company's managers to determine the role of an IT system within an organization. They research the newest technologies and determine if new software or hardware should be implemented. They prepare reports on the costs and benefits of computer upgrades. They design and develop new computing systems, choose appropriate and necessary hardware and software, and make sure computer systems meet company needs.

*Work Environment:* Computer systems analysts work in all industries. They can work for an organization

A computer analyst examines a company's server. Determining the best hardware and software for a business or organization is part of a computer analyst's job.

or an outside consulting firm hired by a company. Typically, they work in offices but many travel to visit worksites where they analyze on-site computing capabilities.

*Educational Requirements:* Most analysts have a bachelor's degree in computer science, computer programming, or information technology. However, some firms may hire analysts with business or liberal arts degrees who know how to write computer programs. It is common for computer programming skills to be self-taught, however formal degree programs may set you apart from your peers and greatly expand your knowledge base and expertise. These programs include courses in computer science theory, programming languages, data management, computer systems, software engineering, algorithms, intelligence systems, and mathematics.

*Career Advancement:* With experience and an advanced degree, systems analysts can grow into positions of leadership within an organization. Project managers lead a team of analysts. Information technology (IT) directors or chief technology officers oversee an entire organization's computing needs, manage analysts, and take on an important leadership role within a company.

## Multimedia Animators

*Job Description:* Multimedia artists and animators create animation and visual effects for a wide range of media projects, from television shows and films to video games and websites.

Multimedia animators use design software to create two- and three-dimensional animations for products, commercials, video games, television shows, and movies.

*Duties and Responsibilities:* Multimedia animators create two- and three-dimensional graphics and animation using computer programs and illustrations. They work with other animators and artists to create

movies, games, or visual effects. They conduct research to ensure their designs are accurate and realistic. They plot out scenes in which animation is used, and they assist in editing animation and effects based on feedback from the project's director, game designer, or client.

*Work Environment:* The overwhelming majority of multimedia animators, roughly 65 percent, are self-employed. This means they own their own companies or freelance for film studios or gaming companies. Most work in offices on computers that are equipped with extensive design software.

*Educational Requirements:* Employers in this profession do not require a degree. Instead, they look for an outstanding portfolio of design and illustration work. Many animators do pursue an associate's or bachelor's degree in computer graphics, animation, multimedia design, new media design, or a related field. Within these programs, students learn design principles, graphic simulation, media interface, new media design, illustration and drawing skills, object and character creation, animation production, film techniques, and stop-motion techniques.

# YOUNG DEVELOPERS THRIVE

Paul Dunahoo runs a small company called Bread and Butter Software, LLC. Among many other business trips, he was recently invited to attend Apple's prestigious Worldwide Developer Conference in San Francisco, California, to meet other developers and to submit his work for critique. While he is best known for creating the first note-taking app, called Scrawl, Dunahoo faces a unique challenge most other chief executive officers (CEOs) don't. He balances the running of his company with attendance at middle school. Dunahoo is only thirteen years old.

Dunahoo isn't a rarity in the app world. Nick D'Aloisio, a sixteen-year-old from South London, launched a popular e-mail and website summarizing application called Summly, which recently attracted the attention of the investors behind Facebook and Spotify. Thomas Suarez of Manhattan Beach, California, created an iOS game called Bustin Jieber, a Whack-a-Mole style game that has players bopping the head of pop star Justin Bieber. Suarez, a sixth grader, recently gave a talk about his creation at TEDxManhattanBeach, an event linked to TED, the nonprofit organization that is devoted to spreading ideas in the fields of technology, entertainment, and design.

Apple has reported that for the last several years it has received thousands of e-mails from teenage developers who have already launched several apps and who are interested in attending the Worldwide Developer Conference. These teens represent a growing group of developers who spend their free time learning how to code for operating systems like Apple's iOS.

Previously, only developers over the age of eighteen were allowed to register for the conference. But now, because some of these younger teenagers are launching exciting and popular apps, Apple has extended an invitation to take part in the conference to developers as young as thirteen years old.

According to the *Wall Street Journal*, teens represent a growing subsection of developers who are learning to build apps. They are either self-taught or they enroll in summer programming classes that are offered by organizations such as the ID Tech Camps, in California, that provide courses in programming, authoring languages, user interface, and design.

*Additional Training:* Some animation studios have created their own in-house software and computer applications. In this case, you will be trained on their software.

*Internships/Co-op Opportunities:* The field is competitive, so any prior experience in animation and multimedia is a plus. This can be accomplished through an internship or co-op program with an animation studio or multimedia design firm. These opportunities will give you hands-on experience working on actual animation projects, and your work can be used to build your professional portfolio.

## Software Developers

*Job Description:* Software developers create computer programs. They are usually in charge of the entire development process for a software program. First,

Google software engineer Greg Millam works at his desk in Washington State. Software developers are employed by major international corporations, such as Google, and by smaller, regional firms.

developers meet with clients to determine how they plan to use the software. Then they design the program and instruct programmers on the desired outcome. Programmers write and test the code per a developer's specifications.

*Duties and Responsibilities:* A software developer talks to users and determines their needs. They design, test, and develop software to accomplish their client's goals. They make recommendations on computer hardware and software upgrades and can even design applications and systems to work together. They maintain software by making sure that it's working correctly and that new versions are updated in a timely manner.

*Work Environment:* Many developers work for software publishers. Developers work full time, and long hours are normal. Nearly all work at desks on computers with sophisticated computer hardware and software.

*Educational Requirements:* Software developers must have a bachelor's degree in computer science and strong computer-programming skills. Computer science degrees cover courses in computer science theory, probability and statistics, calculus, programming languages, database management, algorithms, and intelligent systems.

*Required Skills and Training:* Developers must be good leaders and have strong team management skills. They must be able to communicate the clients' wants and needs to programmers and delegate tasks accordingly. Because they deal with clients on a regular basis, developers should be adept at customer service skills. They should also be detail oriented.

# CHAPTER SIX

# Better Living Through Science and Technology

Scientific and technological advancements are a fundamental part of our future. The impact of technology on the world of science has been overwhelming. We face unprecedented challenges as a nation and planet. From genetic engineering, energy production, population growth, and global warming to nanotechnology, pharmaceutical development, medical advancements, imaging and astronomy, and space exploration, there has never been a more exciting time to embark on a technology career in the sciences.

## Science and Technology Careers

Careers in science and technology allow you to explore the multiple ways that science, technology, and innovation provide solutions to everyday problems. A wide range of industries—including medicine, health care, biomedical research, engineering, bio-technology, aerospace, physics, and alternative ener-gies—combine science and technology.

# Diagnostic Medical Sonographers

*Job Description:* A diagnostic medical sonographer uses imaging equipment to direct sound waves into a patient's body, producing images of body parts in order to assess or diagnose various medical conditions.

*Duties and Responsibilities:* Diagnostic medical sonographers prepare patients for procedures, pre-pare and maintain imaging equipment, use imaging equipment to obtain diagnostic images of a patient's body, detect normal and abnormal conditions, analyze images to provide preliminary findings for physicians, and maintain patients' records.

*Work Environment:* Diagnostic medical sonogra-phers perform most of their work in dimly lit rooms, but some may perform procedures at patients' bed-sides or in emergency rooms. The vast majority of sonographers work in health care facilities.

*Educational Requirements:* Diagnostic medical sonographers need an associate's degree or a postsec-ondary certificate in the field. Associate's degrees and bachelor's degrees are available in diagnostic medical sonography. For those who already have a background in the health field, such as nurses, one-year certificate programs can help bridge the educational gap and prepare health care professionals for a career change within the field.

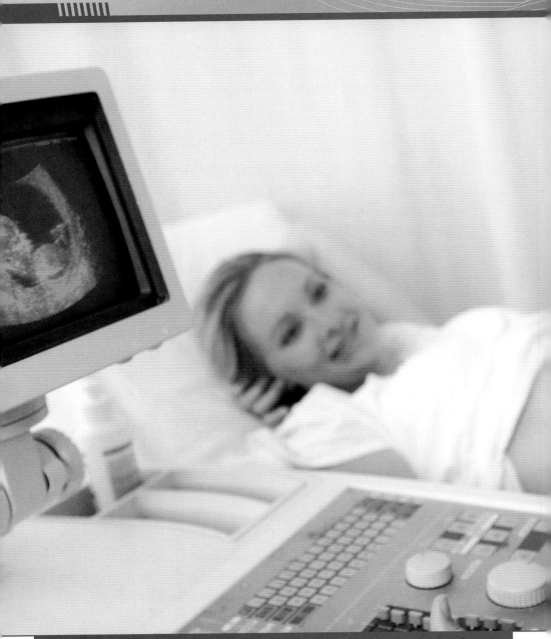

Diagnostic medical sonographers use ultrasound technology to check the health of a developing fetus, assess the extent of internal injuries, and analyze damage to major organs.

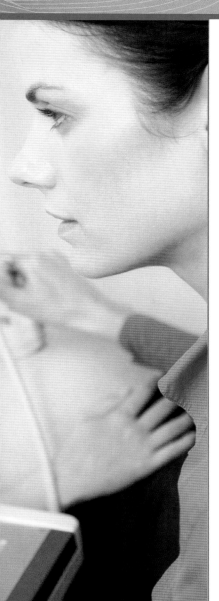

Diagnostic medical sonography programs include course work and clinical training. Course work focuses on biology, anatomy and physiology, sonographic scanning skills and techniques, sonography equipment and instrumentation, patient care, and medical terminology. Clinical rotations give hands-on experience performing sonograms in medical facilities.

*Required Skills and Training:* Diagnostic medical sonographers need excellent hand-eye coordination, strong interpersonal communication skills, and excellent attention to detail.

*Certifications/Licensures:* Many employers prefer sonographers who hold a professional certification, which can be obtained by graduating from an accredited program and passing an exam.

## Geoscientists

*Job Description:* Geoscientists study the physical aspects of the earth. They analyze its composition, structure, and processes to learn about its past, present, and future.

*Duties and Responsibilities:* Geoscientists design and conduct field studies. They visit parts of our planet to collect and evaluate water, air, rock, and soil samples. They review and analyze aerial photographs and other data to locate and estimate the size of natural resource deposits. They produce geologic maps and charts, prepare written reports, and present their findings to fellow scientists and other groups.

*Work Environment:* Geoscientists split their time between fieldwork and offices or laboratories. Geoscientists do travel a lot, often to remote locations all over the world. Due to the prominence of the oil and gas industry, nearly 30 percent of geoscientists are employed in Texas.

*Educational Requirements:* At minimum, a bachelor's degree is required for entry-level positions in the field. For high-level

research work, a doctorate (Ph.D.) is required. Bachelor's degrees in geosciences are most common, though candidates with degree in physics, biology, or chemistry are often acceptable if they have course work in geology. Most geosciences programs are heavily focused on mathematics, computer science,

A geoscientist takes samples of water and ice from a glacier to determine the age and composition of the planet.

and the physical sciences. Course work includes mineralogy, petrology, and structural geology.

*Certifications/Licensures:* Some states require geoscientists to be licensed. Requirements vary by state, but most require a minimum level of education, work experience, and the successful completion of an exam.

*Co-op Opportunities:* A geology co-op provides practical experience to students who wish to pursue professional positions in the geosciences. Many co-op students work as research assistants, data analysts, laboratory assistants, or field assistants for natural gas and energy companies, mining or petroleum operations, research institutes, and government agencies.

## SEVEN UNUSUAL CAREER PATHS IN SCIENCE AND TECHNOLOGY

- **Ethical hacker:** Hackers are usually known for being malicious, stealing sensitive information, or causing massive disruption to computer systems. But an ethical hacker breaks into computer systems for a good cause: to figure out ways to prevent information theft and to develop the newest innovations in cyber security.
- **Chief sustainability officer:** This multidisciplinary career requires knowledge of business, leadership, science, and sustainability. As a chief sustainability officer, you'll lead your organization in making more environmentally friendly business decisions, greener production processes, or more energy-efficient practices.

- **Food chemist:** Sugar-free chocolate, delicious frozen meals, fresher packaged food—as a food chemist, you'll experiment with the chemical makeup of foods to make them tastier, longer lasting, or easier to ship.
- **UX designer/developer:** UX, which stands for "user experience," is how a person interacts with a website, a control panel on a car, or a remote control for the television. A UX designer/developer takes into account how people act intuitively when it comes to electronics. They use that information to develop ways for people to use technology more easily and successfully.
- **Science and technology policy analyst:** Analysts help shape science and technology-related public policies by analyzing how regulatory measures, laws, and funding affect the field.
- **Storm tracker:** Investigate the science of storms by gathering information on severe weather occurrences, including hurricanes, tornadoes, thunderstorms, and flash floods. Storm trackers follow storms in high-tech vehicles fitted with computer equipment designed to measure air pressure, wind speed and direction, water levels, the energy of lightning, and more.
- **Robotics engineer:** Robots explore the depths of the ocean, measure weather at the highest of altitudes, assist in the production of automobiles, and entertain people in amusement parks. Robotics incorporates some of the latest technological innovations.

# Meteorologists (Atmospheric Scientists)

*Job Description:* Meteorologists, also called atmospheric scientists, study weather, climate, and other

Meteorologists track developing storm systems to keep the public informed of regular weather occurrences, such as rain or snow, but also of less frequent weather patterns, such as hurricanes and tornadoes.

aspects of the atmosphere. They analyze weather movement and forecast weather and climate events.

*Duties and Responsibilities:* Meteorologists measure temperature, air pressure, and other properties of the atmosphere to determine how weather will move

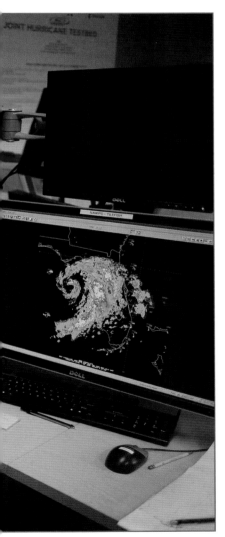

and act over a period of time. They develop and use computer models that track data about the atmosphere, produce maps of where weather may occur, report on current and future weather conditions, and issue warnings to the public to alert them to when and where severe weather can occur. They also use sophisticated computer and mathematical models, satellite images, and radar data to prepare reports and predict long-term weather forecasts.

*Work Environment:* While most people recognize their "weatherman" or "weatherwoman" from local news broadcasts, television stations employ very few meteorologists. Most are employed by the federal government at the National Weather Service (part of the National Oceanic and Atmospheric Administration, or NOAA), the U.S. Department of Defense, or one of the branches of the armed forces. Most work in offices with high-tech computer systems, satellite feeds, and radar. Some travel to where extreme weather conditions are happening to gather data or report from the field.

*Educational Requirements:* Meteorologists need a bachelor's degree in atmospheric science or a related scientific field to begin a career in the field. These programs provide students with a broad background in meteorology, mathematics, computer science, physics, and chemistry. Courses cover topics such as climatology, weather analysis and forecasting, atmospheric thermodynamics, atmospheric physics and remote sensing, meteorological instrumentation, and operational forecasting and weathercasting.

*Required Skills and Training:* Meteorologists need exceptional communication skills to relay complex information to the public in easily understandable ways. For those who appear on news broadcasts, skills in public speaking, voice and diction, and presentation are key.

## Agricultural and Food Scientists

*Job Description:* Agricultural and food scientists maintain the nation's food supply. They work to ensure agricultural productivity and food safety as they work to improve the quality, quantity, and safety of agricultural products.

*Duties and Responsibilities:* Agricultural and food scientists spend much of their time conducting research and experiments on animal nutrition and field

Oregon State University food scientists study berry quality following freezing and thawing. Food scientists test foods to ensure their safety for public consumption.

crops to develop new ways to improve the quantity and quality of produce and farm animals. They assist in creating new food products and develop improved methods for processing, packaging, and delivering food to consumers. They also share their research findings with farmers, state and federal agencies, food producers, and the public.

*Work Environment:* Agricultural and food scientists work in offices, laboratories, and in the field, where they gather data. They often visit farms, food processing plants, or production facilities.

*Educational Requirements:* Agricultural and food scientists need at least a bachelor's degree to enter the field. Degree programs in agricultural science, agricultural production, agricultural technology, animal science, or horticulture provide students with a background in the business and production aspects of the agricultural industry. Course work in these programs covers topics such as biology, chemistry, botany, animal reproduction, livestock management, genetics, food chemistry, food analysis, food microbiology, food engineering, and food processing operations.

*Certifications/Licensures:* Though not a requirement to enter the field, agricultural and food scientists can earn certifications from organizations like the American Registry of Professional Animal Scientists or the Soil Science Society of America. These certifications can enhance the status of those who work in the field.

# You're Hired!
## Landing Your First Technology Job

When you're ready to begin applying for your first job in the technology field, you'll need to be prepared with a job search strategy. This includes drafting a résumé, identifying available positions, networking with professionals, and preparing for interviews.

## Create a Résumé

Before you begin your job search, you need a well-written, well-designed résumé that highlights your skills and abilities. Your résumé is the first impression you make on a potential hiring manager, so it needs to be well crafted. Your résumé needs to tell a potential employer about your work experience, education, skills, special abilities, and any awards or recognition you've earned along the way.

Your résumé should be organized into sections (education, experience, skills recognition, etc.), and each section should be easy to read. Most vocational schools, community colleges, and four-year colleges and universities have career services offices that can assist you in organizing your information and creating a résumé.

For some technology jobs, such as those in animation, graphic design, Web design and development, or gaming, a professional portfolio is needed to illustrate your creative abilities. You can create an online portfolio or carry a traditional hard copy version with you to interviews. An online portfolio should feature the following:

- **Your name and a short biography.** This should include your career goals, your education, and any awards you've won for your creative work.

- **Your work.** Potential employers will want to see what you've accomplished to judge if your style and knowledge fit with their needs and expectations. Your portfolio should contain high-quality images of artwork or illustrations, links to the live versions of websites you've designed, live links to any online gaming or multimedia animation you've created, or samples or images of projects you've completed as part of high school or college classes.

- **Recommendations of your work.** Ask teachers or professors to offer their comments on your work. If you've completed work for clients or companies, ask them to write brief recommendations on your behalf.

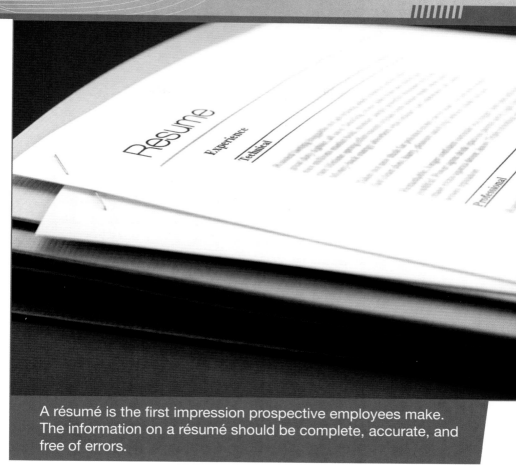

A résumé is the first impression prospective employees make. The information on a résumé should be complete, accurate, and free of errors.

- **Contact information.** Make sure people know how to get a hold of you. Include your mailing address, phone number (landline and cell), and e-mail address.

## Searching for a Job

Searching for a job can be an exciting time in your life. It's an opportunity to identify what you'd like to do and where you'd like to work. Rarely are jobs posted

# MAKE THE WEB WORK FOR YOU

The Internet has become one of the most valuable tools in searching for a job. You can identify open positions on job search and company websites, research potential employers, and seek out advice on everything from effective résumé writing to the best ways to answer typical interview questions. You can even connect to potential employers on career networking sites like LinkedIn. To take advantage of all that the Internet has to offer, you need to adopt a few surefire strategies:

- **Search yourself:** There is such a thing as bad publicity. Hiring managers will search for you on the Internet, so you need to check your own cyber identity. If you've posted inappropriate photos or controversial opinions, or have participated in offensive events, a simple search for your name will produce all of it. And it can turn off a potential employer. Before you start sending out résumés, clean up your cyber image. Remove anything that appears online that you're not comfortable with potential employers seeing.
- **Be your own publicist:** Are there opportunities to promote yourself online that you aren't taking advantage of? Update your LinkedIn profile, use Facebook and other social media sites to drive traffic to your online portfolio of work, and create a professional website that focuses on your accomplishments.
- **Network:** Use LinkedIn or other professional online networks to reach out to professionals in your field. Build contacts, seek advice, and ask a seasoned

professional to mentor you. You can also ask former employers to post professional recommendations and references.

- **Strategize online job applications:** It's easy to upload your résumé to every job you find online and hit send, but that may not be the best strategy. Consider quality over quantity. Tailor your résumé to the job postings that interest you most, and customize each cover letter by researching each company. Hiring managers can tell when you've put in the extra effort.

- **Say thank you:** It's easy to send out a quick e-mail thanking a hiring manager for an interview, but before you do, consider making the gesture more personal. A handwritten note expressing your appreciation is much more impressive and memorable than an e-mail.

in newspapers anymore. Now, almost every company posts open positions on its own website or uses industry or general job search sites to announce vacancies. Searching the Internet for a job can seem like looking for a needle in a haystack, but you need to know how and where to look to find the best positions.

- **Search your niche.** Spend time searching the websites of companies in your area of interest. You can also look to see if an industry has a dedicated employment website. For example, a host of jobs are listed on PackagingCareers.com, an all-encompassing website dedicated to connecting packaging science professionals to jobs in the packaging industry.

Samples of similar sites are available in the fields of meteorology (visit www.nwas.org, the National Weather Association website), diagnostics medical sonography (www.ultrasoundjobs.com), sustainability (jobs.greenbiz.com or www.sustainablebusiness.com), information technology (www.itjobs.com), and more.

- **Post your résumé.** Use industry websites or the job boards of professional organizations to post your résumé. Hiring managers often search these sites to identify candidates who meet the initial requirements of open positions.

- **Create a candidate profile.** Many company websites feature career pages where you can complete a profile about your job interests, credentials, experiences, and salary requirements. If positions open up that match your profile, you may receive a notification that an opening has been posted. Sometimes a hiring manager will contact you directly.

- **Sign up for job alerts and RSS feeds.** You can sign up to receive job alerts or RSS feeds from industry websites that will notify you when new positions are posted in your area of interest.

- **Use filters.** Filters help you weed out the information you don't need so you receive only the most pertinent, relevant, and targeted information from a website. Use filters to select only the job categories and positions for which you qualify and in which you are interested.

# TIPS FOR A SUCCESSFUL INTERVIEW

- **Plan ahead.** Research the company you are interviewing with to learn as much as possible about who they are, what they do, what types of products they make, and who their competitors are. Review your résumé. Think about each of your educational and professional experiences so you are prepared to answer questions about what you learned and how you might adapt those skills to the position you are applying for.

- **Eye contact.** Make eye contact with your interviewer when you answer questions. It shows your interest in the job and in the person with whom you're speaking.

- **Be positive.** Don't speak negatively about past employers, clients, or duties.

- **Listen.** Be aware of what the interviewer is saying about his or her company and the job for which you are interviewing. Ask follow-up questions to show you are engaged in the conversation, listening to what is being said, and interested in the company and the job.

- **Focus on your achievements.** In answering an interviewer's questions, try to provide information that demonstrates what you know and how you would adapt your knowledge to particular situations in this office.

# Preparing for an Interview

Landing a job is all about the interview. While your résumé can highlight your abilities, education, and experience in the field, it doesn't tell a hiring manager

An interview is an opportunity for job seekers to highlight their abilities and strengths. Interviewees should research employers in order to ask specific questions about the company's products, services, and day-to-day operations.

if you have the right personality for the company, if you'll fit in well with the staff, or if you'll excel in a particular work environment.

An interview doesn't just allow a company to learn about you, it's also an opportunity for you to learn about a company. An interview should be a conversation that enables you to assess if this is the type of place you want to be. An employer may be looking for the person who best fits in with his or her staff, but, as an applicant, you should be trying to find out if a company is right for you. An interview is the best way to determine more about both a job and a company.

In an interview, applicants should always act professionally. Turn off your cell phone, don't chew gum or mints while speaking, avoid bringing drinks in to the interview, and make sure to dress professionally. Plan to arrive early for the interview, especially if the location of the office is unfamiliar. If possible, drive to the location ahead of time to map out where you'll park and how to get into the building. Large companies can have multiple parking lots and numerous buildings. The last thing you want to do is begin an interview flustered after arriving late.

# Your First Job

Congratulations, you've landed your first job! Now the real work begins. Your first job is an opportunity to learn from seasoned professionals in your field of interest. It's a time to put yourself out there and soak up as much knowledge as you can. It's also a time when you will begin to learn a lot about the professional world that you can't learn in college classes or from textbooks. While you are working at your first job, remember these tips:

• Your first job is just that: the first in a long line of opportunities you will have. Your first job doesn't predict the future of your career, nor does it teach you all you need to know. It's an opportunity to begin your career. You'll change jobs, maybe even career fields, over the course of your professional life.

• Your attitude is as important as the work you do. One of the biggest complaints about first-time employees is that they often expect more responsibility than they are truly prepared for and they tend to think they know more than seasoned employees. Your first job is a time for you to soak up as much as you can. You have to learn the ropes and earn respect before you begin getting more important assignments.

- Every company, division, department, and office has politics. Learn how decisions are made, who calls the shots, and who has influence.

- Each organization has its own culture that comes through in behaviors and actions. Find out what the company stands for and learn if there are unwritten rules of etiquette.

- You're in charge of your career, not your company. It used to be that a company took responsibility for moving you along a career path. Now, it's up to you to build your skills, take the initiative, and contribute to the company. The knowledge you learn will serve you well as you get promoted. Or, if you decide to leave, you'll take that knowledge and experience with you.

- Don't wait for compliments. If you want to know how you are doing, ask for feedback. Schedule periodic meetings with your direct supervisors to inquire about how you work performance is perceived and if you are producing high-quality work. Seek constructive criticism on how to improve and ask how you can do better. You should always have an accurate idea of how well you are meeting your employer's expectations.

# CHAPTER EIGHT

# Getting Ahead:
## Forging a Lifelong Career in Technology

Technology is ever changing. It is constantly adapted in new ways and, as a result, new career fields emerge at a constant rate. Ten years ago, medical records were kept in paper files in doctors' offices. Now they are entirely online and accessible by medical professionals around the world. Fifteen years ago people were just learning what the Internet was. No one knew that the World Wide Web would soon completely revolutionize the way we shop, read, get news and information, search for jobs, listen to music, and communicate with each other. Technology will continue to evolve, so those who make a commitment to lifelong learning will excel in the STEM fields.

Technology has increased the pace of our lives. We learn something new each day just to keep current in the workplace. While on-the-job training is beneficial, you can't rely on your company or organization to provide you with the education you need to do your job. You need to seek out opportunities to continue to advance your knowledge and skills in your career field.

# Earn an Advanced Degree

An advanced degree is an academic program of study beyond a bachelor's degree. Associate's and bachelor's degrees are two- and four-year programs, respectively, that focus on establishing a solid foundation of general knowledge in a course of study or field of endeavor. Graduate degrees offer in-depth study of a very specific and specialized area of study within a particular field or industry. Undergraduate degrees are a requirement for admission to a graduate degree, and graduate course work builds on the foundation created by the undergraduate degree.

Getting a graduate degree is an excellent way to advance in your career field. A graduate degree will teach you new skills that will help to set you apart from others in your profession. As you learn more advanced knowledge and skills, you'll be better prepared to take on more complex projects at work. You'll also be valued more for your knowledge and advanced level of training. Advanced degrees provide you with an opportunity to hone your knowledge in a specific area of your industry. Professionals with specialized knowledge or training in a particular field will automatically be valued more in the workplace. Specialization also allows you

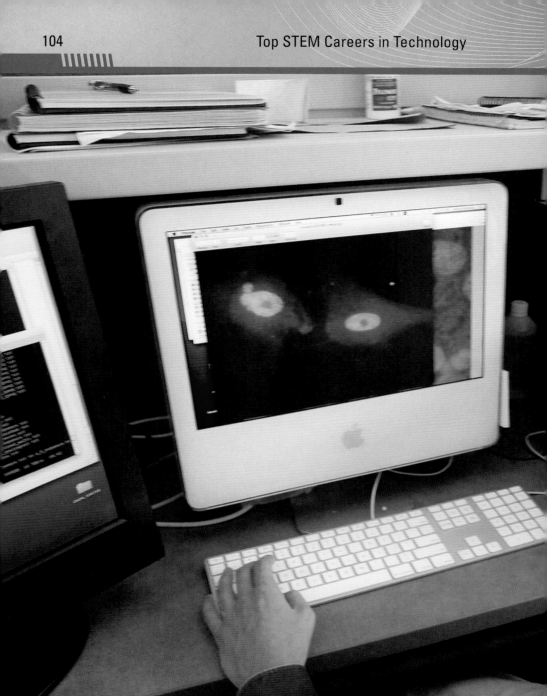

A Ph.D. candidate in Connecticut examines stem-cell images. Advanced degrees can provide workers with in-depth knowledge in their field and can also lead to career advancement.

to establish yourself as an expert in a particular subject. You will also earn a higher salary with an advanced degree. A recent study showed that biology and life science majors with graduate degrees earned 70 percent more than those with only bachelor's degrees in the same field.

## Follow Advancements in Your Field

Keep tabs on the innovations taking place in your career field. How is technology being used to change how you do your daily work? Are there ways you can implement new procedures that will save time and money? Find out what's happening so you can share the information with others at your company. New research that has the potential to change how you do your job is emerging daily in numerous industries.

# SCIENCE AND TECHNOLOGY ADVANCEMENTS TO WATCH

- **Stem cell heart generation:** For the first time in medical history, a human heart has been created using stem cells. The implications of this development are enormous. It's a giant step forward in the evolution of organ generation, and it can also help patients awaiting heart transplants.
- **Hybrid MRI/PET imaging:** Engineers and medical imaging scientists are working toward creating a simultaneous positron emission tomography (PET) and magnetic resonance imaging (MRI) image that could provide a broad and extensive level of diagnosis for medical conditions. The combination of these two types of imaging means both the soft tissue and structural analysis of a body can be performed.
- **Paperless paper:** Soon there may be a product that looks and feels like paper but has the advantages of a digital device. While the technology is already available, it hasn't yet been used to create a product for consumers to buy at their local tech store. Paperless paper has the potential to have an enormously positive impact on the environment. Trees and lumber can be preserved instead of cut down to manufacture traditional paper.
- **Ocean desalination:** As our natural resources continue to decline, more efforts are being put into creating ways to make ocean water safer to drink. Ocean desalination is the removal of salt from ocean water to make it drinkable.

Attendees arrive for a 2011 biotechnology convention in Washington, D.C. Conferences offer professional and personal networking opportunities.

# Attend Industry Conferences

Nearly all industries have professional organizations dedicated to sharing the latest information, advancements, and innovations occurring in the field. Join your industry's professional organization and attend regional, state, and national conferences. Not only will you meet people in your career field who may become a valuable part of your professional network, you'll also obtain the latest information about emerging technologies affecting your field. You'll be able to bring this knowledge back to your company and apply what you've learned to improve the way you do things.

# GLOSSARY

**ACCREDITATION** A process in which certification of competency, authority, or credibility is presented.

**ANALYST** A person who reviews data and information.

**CAPITAL** Another term for money or funding.

**DNA** Deoxyribonucleic acid (DNA); a molecule that encodes the genetic instructions used in the development and functioning of all known living organisms.

**ECOSYSTEM** A community of living organisms.

**ENTREPRENEUR** An individual who organizes and operates a business or businesses, taking on financial risk to do so.

**ERGONOMICS** The applied science of equipment design, as for the workplace.

**HYDRAULICS** A topic in applied science and engineering dealing with the mechanical properties of liquids.

**INNOVATION** The act of introducing something new.

**MENTOR** An experienced or trusted adviser.

**MINORITY** The smaller in number of two groups constituting a whole; a part of a population differing from others in some characteristics and often subjected to differential treatment; a member of a minority group.

**PATENT LAW** A set of exclusive rights granted by a sovereign state to an inventor or his or her assignee for a limited period of time.

**PHARMACEUTICAL** A medicine or medication; of, relating to, or engaged in pharmacy or the manufacture and sale of pharmaceuticals.

**PNEUMATICS** An area of technology that deals with the study and application of pressurized gas to produce mechanical motion.

**POLLUTION** The introduction of contaminants that cause adverse change into the natural environment.

**REMEDIATION** The act or process of correcting a fault or deficiency.

**RSS** Short for really simple syndication, it is a family of Web feed formats designed to allow frequent updating of information, such as with blog posts, news headlines and updates, and Web feeds.

**STATISTICS** The study of the collection, organization, analysis, interpretation, and presentation of data.

**SUSTAINABILITY** The capacity to endure.

# FOR MORE INFORMATION

American Meteorological Society
45 Beacon Street
Boston, MA 02108-3693
(617) 227-2425
Website: http://www.ametsoc.org
This society promotes the development and dissemination of information relating to the atmospheric and related oceanic and hydrologic sciences.

Association of Information Technology Professionals
330 North Wabash Avenue, Suite 2000
Chicago, IL 60611
(800) 224-9371
Website: http://www.aitp.org
This association provides leadership and educational opportunities through partnerships with industry, government, and academia.

Biomedical Engineering Society (BMES)
8201 Corporate Drive, Suite 1125
Landover, MD 20785-2224
(301) 459-1999
Website: http://bmes.org
The BMES is one of the world's leading professional organizations devoted to developing and using engineering and technology to advance human health and well-being.

Center for International Science and Technology Policy
1957 E Street NW, Suite 403
Washington, DC 20052

(202) 994.7292
Website: http://www.gwu.edu/~cistp
The Center for International Science and Technology
    Policy is a world leader in international public policy
    research and education in science, technology,
    and innovation.

Earthwatch
114 Western Avenue
Boston, MA 02134
(800) 776-0188
Website: http://www.earthwatch.org
Earthwatch's mission is to engage people worldwide in
    scientific field research and education in order to
    promote the understanding and action necessary
    for a sustainable environment.

Institute of Electrical and Electronics Engineers (IEEE)
2001 L Street NW, Suite 700
Washington, DC 20036-4910
(202) 785-001
Website: http://www.ieeeusa.org
IEEE's core purpose is to foster technological innova-
    tion and excellence for the benefit of humanity.

Women in Technology International (WITI)
Olympic Plaza
11500 Olympic Boulevard, Suite 400
Los Angeles, CA 90064
(818) 788-9484

Website: http://www.witi.com

WITI's mission is to empower women worldwide to achieve unimagined possibilities and transformations through technology, leadership, and economic prosperity.

World Packaging Organisation
1833 Centre Point Circle, Suite 123
Naperville, IL 60563
(630) 596-9007
Website: http://www.worldpackaging.org

The World Packaging Organisation is a nonprofit international federation of national packaging institutes and associations that encourages and fosters education and training in packaging.

# Websites

Due to the changing nature of Internet links, Rosen Publishing has developed an online list of websites related to the subject of this book. This site is updated regularly. Please use this link to access the list:

http://www.rosenlinks.com/STEM/Tech

Bastas, Sideris. *Teens and Technology: What Makes Your Teen Tick and How to Keep Them Safe*. Frederick, MD: PublishAmerica, 2009.

Cater-Steel, Aileen, and Emily Cater. *Women in Engineering, Science, and Technology: Education and Career Challenges*. Hershey, PA: Engineering Science Reference, 2010.

Cindrich, Sharon, and Ali Douglass. *A Smart Girl's Guide to the Internet*. Middleton, WI: American Girl, 2009.

Cook, David. *Robot Building for Beginners* (Technology in Action). New York, NY: Apress, 2010.

Evans, Alan, Kendall Martin, and Mary Anne Poatsy. *Technology In Action*. Lebanon, IN: Prentice Hall, 2012.

Farrell, Mary E. *Computer Programming for Teens*. Independence, KY: Cengage Learning PTR, 2007.

Ford, Jerry Lee, Jr. *Scratch Programming for Teens*. Independence, KY: Cengage Learning PTR, 2008.

Harbour, Jonathan S. *Video Game Programming for Kids*. Independence, KY: Cengage Learning PTR, 2007.

Jackson, Barbara J. *Construction Management JumpStart: The Best First Step Toward a Career in Construction Management*. Hoboken, NJ: Wiley-Sybex, 2010.

Kalpakjian, Serope, and Steven Schmid. *Manufacturing Engineering & Technology*. Lebanon, IN: Prentice Hall, 2009.

Layne, Margaret E. *Women in Engineering: Professional Life*. Reston, VA: American Society of Civil Engineers, 2009.

Montgomery, Sy, and Temple Grandin. *Temple Grandin: How the Girl Who Loved Cows Embraced*

*Autism and Changed the World*. New York, NY: HMH Books for Young Readers, 2012.

Morgan, George D., and Ashley Stroup. *Rocket Girl: The Story of Mary Sherman Morgan, America's First Female Rocket Scientist*. Amherst, NY: Prometheus Books, 2013.

Pond, Robert J., and Jeffrey L. Rankinen. *Introduction to Engineering Technology*. Lebanon, IN: Prentice Hall, 2008.

Purcell, Karen. *Unlocking Your Brilliance: Smart Strategies for Women to Thrive in Science, Technology, Engineering, and Math*. Austin, TX: Greenleaf Book Group Press, 2012.

Ripley, Amanda. *The Smartest Kids in the World: And How They Got That Way*. New York, NY: Simon & Schuster, 2013.

Rosser, Sue V. *Breaking into the Lab: Engineering Progress for Women in Science*. New York, NY: NYU Press, 2012.

Sande, Warren, and Carter Sande. *Hello World! Computer Programming for Kids and Other Beginners*. Shelter Island, NY: Manning Publications, 2009.

Wagner, Tony. *Creating Innovators: The Making of Young People Who Will Change the World*. New York, NY: Scribner, 2012.

Wright, R. Thomas. *Technology & Engineering*. Tinley Park, IL: Goodheart-Willcox, 2011.

# BIBLIOGRAPHY

ABET.org. "Engineering vs. Engineering Technology." August 2013 (http://www.abet.org/engineering-vs-engineering-technology).

Agarwal, Nirmala. "What Are the Adverse Effects of Technology on Our Environment?" PreserveArticles .com. Retrieved August 2013 (http://www.preserve articles.com/201101052550/adverse-effects-of-technology-on-our-environment.html).

American Intercontinental University. "The Importance of Lifelong Learning." Retrieved August 2013 (http://info.aiuonline.edu/aiuzine/issue31/theme1.asp).

Association for Computing Machinery. "Top 10 Reasons to Major in Computing." Retrieved August 2013 (http://computingcareers.acm.org/?page_id=4).

Bardaro, Katie. "Numbers: Not Just for Math Majors Anymore." *New York Times*, March 25, 2013. Retrieved August 2013 (http://www.nytimes .com/roomfordebate/2013/03/24/for-the-college-bound-are-there-any-safe-bets/stem-skills-arent-just-for-stem-majors).

Brooks, Chad. "Women's STEM Careers a Matter of Choice, Not Ability, Study Suggests." Huffington Post, March 21, 2013. Retrieved August 2013 (http://www.huffingtonpost.com/2013/03/21/women-stem-math-science-skills-career_n_2923388.html).

Burnsed, Brian. "Understand the Value of a Graduate Degree." *U.S. News & World Report*, June 27, 2011. Retrieved August 2013 (http://www .usnews.com/education/best-graduate-schools /articles/2011/06/27/understand-the-value-of-a-graduate-degree).

Bybee, Roger W. *The Case for STEM Education: Challenges and Opportunities.* Arlington, VA: National Science Teachers Association, 2013.

Cabot, Heather. "Five Web Tips for Landing Your First Job." Monster.com. Retrieved August 2013 (http://career-advice.monster.com/job-search/getting-started/5-web-tips-for-landing-your-first-job-hot-jobs/article.aspx).

Capraro, Robert M., et al (eds). *STEM Project-Based Learning: An Integrated Science, Technology, Engineering, and Mathematics (STEM) Approach.* Rotterdam, The Netherlands: Sense Publishers, 2013.

Committee on Highly Successful Schools or Programs in K-12 STEM Education. *Successful K–12 STEM Education: Identifying Effective Approaches in Science, Technology, Engineering, and Mathematics.* Washington, DC: National Academies Press, 2011.

Drew, David E. *STEM the Tide: Reforming Science, Technology, Engineering, and Math Education in America.* Baltimore, MD: Johns Hopkins University Press, 2011.

Eberle, Francis. "Why STEM Education Is Important." ISA.org, September/October 2010. Retrieved August 2013 (http://www.isa.org/InTechTemplate.cfm?template=/ContentManagement/ContentDisplay.cfm&ContentID=83593).

EducationPortal.com. "Package Designer: Job Description, Duties, and Requirements." Retrieved August 2013 (http://education-portal.com/articles/Package_Designer_Job_Description_Duties_and_Requirements.html).

Environmental Protection Agency. "What Is Sustainability?" Retrieved August 2013 (http://www.epa.gov/sustainability/basicinfo.htm#sustainability).

FoodAndBeveragePackaging.com. "Heinz Named Food & Beverage Packaging's Food Packager of the Year." September 8, 2011. Retrieved August 2013 (http://www.foodandbeveragepackaging.com/articles/85763-heinz-named-food-beverage-packaging-s-food-packager-of-the-year).

FoundationCenter.org. "Minorities Underrepresented in STEM, Report Finds." October 14, 2010. Retrieved August 2013 (http://foundationcenter.org/pnd/news/story.jhtml?id=310300014).

Hamilton, James. "Careers in Environmental Remediation." BLS.gov. Retrieved August 2013 (http://www.bls.gov/green/environmental_remediation/remediation.htm#professionals).

Harvard magazine. "Cancer Fighting Robots." September/October 2012. Retrieved August 2013 (http://harvardmagazine.com/2012/09/cancer-fighting-robots).

Heining, Andrew. "New Heinz Ketchup Packets Let You Dunk or Squeeze." Christian Science Monitor, February 5, 2010. Retrieved August 2013 (http://www.csmonitor.com/Innovation/Horizons/2010/0205/New-Heinz-ketchup-packets-let-you-dunk-or-squeeze).

Hill, Stephanie C. "Making STEM Cool." Baltimore Sun, August 19, 2013. Retrieved August 2013 (http://www.baltimoresun.com/news/opinion/oped/bs-ed-stem-women-20130819,0,2713528.story#ixzz2d65sZxCR).

Honey, Margaret, and David E. Kanter. *Design, Make, Play: Growing the Next Generation of STEM Innovators*. New York, NY: Routledge, 2013.

Knight, Karen, "Tips for Making the Most of Your First Entry-Level Job." Monster.com. Retrieved August 2013 (http://college.monster.com/benefits/articles/252-tips-for-making-the-most-of-your-first-entry-level-job).

Livadas, Greg. "Personal Watercraft Users Could Save Time and Money." Rochester Institute of Technology, February 11, 2013. Retrieved August 2013 (http://www.rit.edu/news/story.php?id=49733).

McCrea, Bridget. "Engaging Girls In STEM." TheJournal.com, September 8, 2010. Retrieved August 2013 (http://thejournal.com/articles/2010/09/08/engaging-girls-in-stem.aspx).

Moomaw, Sally. *Teaching STEM in the Early Years: Activities for Integrating Science, Technology, Engineering, and Mathematics*. St. Paul, MN: Redleaf Press, 2013.

Moritz, Melissa. "STEM's Most Overlooked Subject: Computer Science." Teach for America, December 14, 2012. Retrieved August 2013 (https://www.teachforamerica.org/blog/stem%E2%80%99s-most-overlooked-subject-computer-science).

Morse, Bob. "Top-Ranked Universities that Grant the Most STEM Degrees." *U.S. News & World Report*, June 18, 2013. Retrieved August 2013 (http://www.usnews.com/education/blogs/college-rankings-blog/2013/06/18/top-ranked-universities-that-grant-the-most-stem-degrees).

NerdGirls.com. "Learn About Nerd Girls." Retrieved August 2013 (http://www.nerdgirls.com).

NiceAngle.com. "What Is Packaging Science?" Retrieved August 2013 (http://www.niceangle.com/Web/whyps.htm).

Oljace, Glory. *STEM Is Elementary: Why Elementary Science, Technology, Engineering, and Mathematics Prepares Students to Beat the Gaps!* Bethel, MN: STEM Is Elementary, LLC, 2012.

Pickard, Vivian R. "As STEM Graduates Rates Decline, Finding and Improving STEM Education Is More Crucial Than Ever." *Huffington Post*, August 12, 2013. Retrieved August 2013 (http://www.huffington post.com/vivian-r-pickard/as-stem-graduate-rates-de_b_3744718.html).

Sauter, Mike. "High-Tech Jobs That Don't Require a College Degree." *USA Today*, July 6, 2013. Retrieved August 2013 (http://www.usatoday.com/story /money/business/2013/07/06/high-tech-jobs-no-college-degree/2487025).

Schiavelli, Mel. "STEM Jobs Outlook Strong, but Collaboration Needed to Fill Jobs." *U.S. News & World Report*, November 3, 2011. Retrieved August 2013 (http://www.usnews.com/news/blogs/stem-education/2011/11/03/stem-jobs-outlook-strong-but-collaboration-needed-to-fill-jobs).

SciencePioneers.org. "Why STEM Education Is Important for Everyone." Retrieved August 2013 (http://www.sciencepioneers.org/parents/why-stem-is-important-to-everyone).

U.S. Bureau of Labor Statistics. "Agricultural and Food Scientists." Retrieved August 2013 (http://www.bls.gov/ooh/life-physical-and-social-science/agricultural-and-food-scientists.htm).

U.S. Bureau of Labor Statistics. "Atmospheric Scientists, including Meteorologists." Retrieved August 2013 (http://www.bls.gov/ooh/life-physical-and-social-science/atmospheric-scientists-including-meteorologists.htm).

U.S. Bureau of Labor Statistics. "Automotive Service Technicians and Mechanics." Retrieved August 2013 (http://www.bls.gov/ooh/installation-maintenance-and-repair/automotive-service-technicians-and-mechanics.htm#tab-4).

U.S. Bureau of Labor Statistics. "Biomedical Engineers." Retrieved August 2013 (http://www.bls.gov/ooh/architecture-and-engineering/biomedical-engineers.htm#tab-2).

U.S. Bureau of Labor Statistics. "Computer System Analysts." Retrieved August 2013 (http://www.bls.gov/ooh/Computer-and-Information-Technology/Computer-systems-analysts.htm).

U.S. Bureau of Labor Statistics. "Diagnostic Medical Sonographers." Retrieve August 2013 (http://www.bls.gov/ooh/health care/diagnostic-medical-sonographers.htm).

U.S. Bureau of Labor Statistics. "Environmental Engineering Technicians." Retrieved August 2013 (http://www.bls.gov/ooh/architecture-and-engineering/environmental-engineering-technicians.htm).

U.S. Bureau of Labor Statistics. "Environmental Scientists and Specialists." Retrieved August 2013 (http://www.bls.gov/ooh/life-physical-and-social-science/environmental-scientists-and-specialists.htm).

U.S. Bureau of Labor Statistics. "Geoscientists." Retrieved August 2013 (http://www.bls.gov/ooh

/life-physical-and-social-science/geoscientists
.htm).

U.S. Bureau of Labor Statistics. "Health and Safety
Engineers." Retrieved August 2013 (http://www
.bls.gov/ooh/architecture-and-engineering/health-
and-safety-engineers.htm).

U.S. Bureau of Labor Statistics. "Hydrologists." Retrieved August 2013 (http://www.bls.gov/ooh/life-
physical-and-social-science/hydrologists.htm).

U.S. Bureau of Labor Statistics. "Industrial Production
Manager." Retrieved August 2013 (http://www
.bls.gov/ooh/management/industrial-production-
managers.htm#tab-4).

U.S. Bureau of Labor Statistics. "Medical Records and
Health Information Technicians." Retrieved August
2013 (http://www.bls.gov/ooh/Healthcare/Medical-
records-and-health-information-technicians.htm).

U.S. Bureau of Labor Statistics. "Multimedia Artists
and Animators." Retrieved August 2013 (http://
www.bls.gov/ooh/arts-and-design/multimedia-
artists-and-animators.htm#tab-4).

U.S. Bureau of Labor Statistics. "Software Developers." Retrieved August 2013 (http://www.bls.gov
/ooh/Computer-and-Information-Technology/
Software-developers.htm).

U.S. Bureau of Labor Statistics. "Surveyors." Retrieved
August 2013 (http://www.bls.gov/ooh/architecture-
and-engineering/surveyors.htm).

Wall Street Journal. "How to Search for a Job Online."
Retrieved August 2013 (http://guides.wsj.com
/careers/how-to-identify-job-opportunities/how-
to-search-for-a-job-online).

# INDEX

# About the Author

Laura La Bella is a writer and editor who has written numerous books on science, technology, engineering, and careers, including *Not Enough to Drink: Pollution, Drought, and Tainted Water Supplies*; *Safety and the Food Supply*; *Careers in Web Development*; *Dream Jobs in Sports Fitness and Medicine*; *Internship and Volunteer Opportunities for People Who Love to Build Things*; and *Careers in Crisis Management and Hostage Negotiation*. La Bella lives in Rochester, New York, with her husband and son.

# Photo Credits

Designer: Brian Garvey; Editor: John Kemmerer;
Photo Researcher: Amy Feinberg